A peek inside the gritty underbelly of the Melbourne police world in the 90's, through the lens of a young female cadet. This book brings the human side of being in law enforcement to light - sharing the personal, sexual, and business life of author, Wilkins as she navigated her first few years in the police force. A humorous and often confronting look at what it is to be a woman in uniform

~ Kym Jackson, Author/Actress

It was like a blast from the past reading Wendy's memoir of her time in the force. The good the bad and the ugly of life as a cop in Melbourne Australia. A nice quick read and thoroughly entertaining read with some wonderful characters.

~AW Ex-Detective Sergeant, Victoria Police

I like the humor and the crime stories it also has a touch of a "clueless fifty shades of Grey"

~ Belinda Gosbee, actress/writer

You wrote the truth about me, at least you changed my name!

- ######

If Sex and The City had a fifth shero, it would certainly be author, actress, real estate entrepreneur, and former cop, Wendy Wilkins, whose novella gives us a dazzling inside look at her smart, sexy, and entertaining life and inspires us to live ours more fully.

- Jaimsyne Blakely Writer, Creator, Innovator

sex, love & cops

Wendy Wilkins

sex, love & cops
© 2018 Wendy Wilkins. All rights reserved.

No part of this book may be reproduced in any form or by any means, electronic, mechanical, digital, photocopying or recording, except for the inclusion in a review, without permission in writing from the publisher.

Published in the USA by:
W Productions Publishing
http://www.wendywilkins.com

Printed in the United States of America
ISBN   978-0-692-14809-9 (paperback)
978-0-578-20720-9 (ebook)

Book design by Darlene Swanson • www.van-garde.com
Cover design by Karis Drake

To all the police around the world
who keep us safe.

And to my family and friends
who support me in all my adventures.

Contents

	Prologue ix	
Chapter 1	The Police Academy. 1	
Chapter 2	Graduation 13	
Chapter 3	Charles "The Sexy Saint" My First True Love 17	
Chapter 4	Charles Returns, The Spell Is Broken and Joe the Vice Cop 27	
Chapter 5	Loss of Love and Innocence A Broken Heart 33	
Chapter 6	My First Week on the Job and First Punch In the Face 37	
Chapter 7	Cops and Prostitutes 49	

Chapter 8	Cops and Guns 61
Chapter 9	Crush on the Detective 73
Chapter 10	Frank and Nightclub Fever 77
Chapter 11	Charlie and I Reunite and My Boyfriend Gets Arrested 81
Chapter 12	Aliens and Cops Playing Pranks. 87
Chapter 13	My Girlfriend the Stripper... and Drugs. . .93
Chapter 14	A Waste of Life 105
Chapter 15	Inappropriate Behavior 113
Chapter 16	Bad Cop 123
Chapter 17	Drunk Drivers and a Cop Goes to Jail . . 127
Chapter 18	My Biggest Arrest 131
Chapter 19	Sliding Doors 137
	Epilogue 141
	About the Author 143

Prologue

I entered through the velvet rope, asking the bouncer if Frank was in tonight. The bouncer nodded a friendly yes. Inside the music was pumping, immediately putting me in the mood to dance. I passed by the general section and made my way up to the VIP area. Frank was holding court with a couple of 'major men about town'. The usual 'hangers on' were standing around, all trying to get a 'piece of' Frank.

Frank, always charming, so good looking, I don't know how he did it every night, making small talk to hundreds of people all wanting a piece of the most connected man in the city. Every celebrity that came into town, he entertained. They all wanted to come to the hottest club in town.

I also happened to be a young cop, fresh out of the Police Academy. I didn't realize until years later what a 'turn on' apparently that was for guys. Something about a woman in uniform... Most men I meet, even until this day, when they find out I was a cop ask me "Do you still have your handcuffs?".

The first time I used mine was on a sixteen year old girl who had spat on me, then tried to kick out the back window of the police car with her heavy boots and screaming, "I want IID". It was interesting that a girl of this young age knew the pseudonym for the police 'Internal Investigations Department'. My memories of handcuffs are not pretty or sexual in any shape or form.

Chapter 1

The Police Academy

It was like boarding school. We all lived in these huge old buildings at the Mt Waverley Police Academy. It was unusual, but we had five girls in our squad of twenty five. Usually there was two or three at the most.

My room mate, Sarah, I thought would make the perfect cop, she was smart, strong, fair and fun, and not taking herself too seriously. We got on well and became close friends.

Recently we caught up again when we happened to both be in London at the same time and I got to meet her beautiful young adult daughter.

Our room was on the 2nd floor, sparse. Two beds one on each side and a desk each, floor boards and a cupboard. We had a large window looking out over the manicured grounds to the front entrance and guard gate.

The boys (our squad mates) were always playing tricks on us. One time we came back to our small room and both our mattresses had disappeared. Another time, I was walking down the hallway and two of my squad mates were walking towards me wearing my one piece bathers over the top of their clothes and doing a mock fashion parade. I was furious, apart from the fact that huge invasions of privacy were occurring, breaking into our room regularly, they were also stretching them and that swimwear fit me perfectly!

John

John was in the squad junior to me, blonde haired, tanned, and a surfer. I couldn't resist his cheeky dimpled smile and cockiness, despite the fact he wasn't tall, he was very confident. They had just lowered height restrictions for cops entry to the police force.

We began stealing kisses and attempting to keep our 'new relationship' under wraps. We had weekends off from the Academy and I remember him taking me home one weekend and meeting his very cool bohemian parents.

The week before, my squad had been on a tour of the morgue to observe our first autopsy. John's father was doing some kind of carpentry work in the back yard and when he turned on the chainsaw I began to feel queasy and explained to John and his parents over lunch that the sound reminded me of the morgue visit the week before when the mortician had taken out a chainsaw and began sawing the skull off a young corpse. The mortician then took the brain out and stuffed the skull back up with newspaper and said "We will sew this back up later".

I also mentioned that "after I got over the first round of queasiness I was quite fascinated to watch this process and that it was funny that three of my male squad mates fainted but none of the girls did." I don't think John's parents thought much of my lunchtime conversation.

John and I got caught kissing once at the Academy and we were written up for an incident report. There is supposed to be no fraternization between trainees in the Academy. If you get three incident reports you can be suspended.

Sarah and I had already had an incident report for not having a clean room. There were spot inspections done regularly and our room *was* clean but not by the standards of the inspector, apparently.

John and I had to stand in front of the Chief Inspector of the Academy, in his office and get a good talking to about proper conduct. We both showed appropriate remorse, but continued to steal kisses whenever we could. After all we were both pretty horny twenty-year-olds.

The Police Academy

One night John was on guard duty and Sarah and I had so much fun calling out to him like ghosts from our window. "Jooohhnnn... Jooohhhnn...." and then hiding under the windowsill. John kept coming out of the guard box, looking around, not seeing anything and going back in. We thought it was hilarious.

I can't remember why John and I broke up, but I do remember it was at my best friend's 21st birthday party, A toga party and John and I had a fight and I chased after him, crying. I remember feeling sorry for myself and not being much of a best friend that night, making it more about me than her party!

Things You Learn In the Academy

The Academy training lasts for nine months and then you are sent to different training stations and various branches of the police force for the following eighteen months and then back to the Academy for a month before you are a fully fledged cop.

You learn all sorts of things in the Academy, you study the law, police procedures etc, the phonetic alphabet, basic firearm training, self defense and we had a course called "Human Behavior" where we had to role play. One day we were divided into groups and one group played the cops, and the other the public, in the park.

I was one of the "members of the public" and we were told to really heckle "the cops". We started yelling out stuff and really got into it including calling out "Here come the pigs" and "I smell bacon".

The group playing the cops asked our instructor if he could instruct our group "to not be so mean" but the instructor just laughed.

The Police Academy

We did lots of physical training including, swimming, long distance running, boxing, basic martial arts, self defense.

One day we were on the soft mats practicing some "self defense" moves when one of the other female trainees in our squad let out an accidental audible fart, close by me and we could not stop laughing.

The instructor said "What's so funny Blondie?" That was the derogatory nickname I was given.

"Nothing Sir", I answered so he made all of us drop and do forty push ups.

We also had to do lots of marching and standing to attention and the instructor would come past and inspect us for things such as our shoes being shiny enough and our uniforms clean and pressed. I was constantly berated for not having my hair bun in a neat enough bun. I must admit this was a difficult task for me to do, to keep all my hair in place. I was also singled out one day for 'wearing too much make up' which was not true as I didn't really wear any in those days.

Our firearms training was pretty basic. The first time I shot my 'Smith and Wesson 38' the first shot went into the police academy ceiling, before I learnt to use it properly.

We were also put through a simulated course of an armed bank robbery, which is a bit like a live video game where good guys and bad guys pop up all over the place, some shooting at you. I only "shot" one civilian.

Studying Crime Scenes...

One of my favorite classes in the Academy was crime scene studies. This class was conducted by a senior level sergeant who showed us various slides and gave us information about what had been found at the crime scene. Our class would ask various questions to help deduce what had occurred and make suggestions on how to go about investigating and solving the crime.

One in particular sticks out in my mind. We were shown a graphic scene. The slide showed a dead naked body of an 85 year old female, spread eagled, face up on her bed, a frozen look of terror and a large wooden hairbrush handle protruding from her vagina. The bedroom showed signs of being ransacked.

The information we were given was that the woman lived alone. There was no sign of forced entry to her ground floor home unit, situated in a middle class suburban neighborhood. The woman was discovered by her daughter who immediately called the police. It was established she had been dead for approximately thirty-six hours. According to her daughter, there did not seem to be any major items stolen.

My immediate thoughts were: 1. I felt sorry for this poor woman who had died in such a horrible way. 2. I felt sorry for the daughter discovering her mother in this tragic way. and 3. Who would rape an 85-year-old woman? Disgusting!

Most of the class, including me, deduced that the woman must have known the perpetrator, hence no forced entry. Or, he did not look particularly threatening and had gained entry by some ruse. For example, offering to help with minor jobs around the house for a small wage. We also deduced that the perpetrator must be disturbed and have major anger issues, re: the jammed hairbrush.

My thoughts swapped back-and-forth between outrage at such a horrible crime, and the excitement of the possibility of being able to make a difference in this world by catching such disgusting criminals and putting them behind bars.

The class asked questions such as, "Have there been any rape cases with the same MO (Motis Operandi) in the area?" "What about fingerprints? Did they match anyone on police files?"

The class became more excited about possibly solving this crime and "putting away" such a horrible aggressive attacker, picking on an elderly woman who lives alone.

The sergeant finally gave us the full details. The woman had in fact died of a heart attack while masturbating using her own hairbrush!

The lesson learned that day? The way something looks may not necessarily be what actually happened.

... Or don't rely on first impressions

David Soon to Be the Detective

I met David, (who became a detective and more about him later) in the Academy. He was in one of the senior squads about to graduate. He made fun of me one time in the huge mess room hall when I walked past his table.

He said "Hey your headlights are on."

I thought to myself "How does he know what car I drive and it's been parked in the car park all week, wouldn't the battery be flat by now?"

I was so naive I didn't realize why all his squad mates were sniggering because the 'headlights' they were referring to were my 'erect nipples'.

If we weren't already qualified with first aid treatment (EMT) we were supposed to attend the St Johns Ambulance training every Wednesday night in the mess hall. All our other training classes were by inspectors and sargeants, our peers in the police force, so a huge amount of deference applied in those classes but with the St.Johns Ambulance training it was extra curricular and a chance to "muck about a bit".

We were put in groups and David who was also doing the class, said, "Come join ours". Then he proceeded to nominate me as the volunteer 'dummy' and took great pleasure in tying me up in bandages. I did not think it was funny at all but everyone else thought it was hilarious.

Chapter 2

Graduation

Our graduation ceremony was a big deal. Two squads of twenty-five graduates each. We were given our badge numbers. These were allocated in consecutive order, according to how we placed over all classes, including the physical training.

Before graduation there was a lot of back and forth chatter. It was rumored that I may be awarded the Dux of the two squads. A rarity for a female, mainly because we couldn't compete as well on the physical side, (generally speaking). I was very athletic in those days and taught high impact aerobics. Yes I wore those Jane Fonda style leotards that split you right up the middle! Though I don't ever remember them being uncomfortable.

It made a small amount of difference what your badge number was. For example, if two cops were applying for the same position at another station, and they were the same rank, then the lower badge number would win the position. It also let other cops know how long you'd been in the force. I still remember my number today which is many thousands less than the current cops' joining today.

With anticipation we waited to hear the results. I graduated in third place overall, which I was very happy with.

We marched in formation and shook hands with the Chief Commissioner in front of our friends and family and threw our hats high into the air. It was a lovely day and I know my family and friends were very proud of me.

My 'twin' brother had been in a major car accident a few weeks before. Some drunken idiot slammed

Graduation

into the back of him. (Some more about drunk drivers later). We were all very worried about him, but he recovered pretty quickly and was able to come to my graduation, though scarred and bandaged, in a wheelchair. He stood up to cheer me when they announced my name. Afterwards, he told me that people close by thought it was a miracle. "He can walk!". My brother had been advised by the doctor not to walk for a few weeks until properly healed, though my darling brother was not going to miss standing up for me.

We had a formal dinner and danced the night away. I was dating the trainee surfer cop, who was graduating a couple of months after me. The romance was short lived, however he came as my date to the formal graduation dinner and got tongues wagging. Most of my squad mates already knew what was going on. A few of the boys stirred him up, saying, "You're not a real cop yet" and "This is not your graduation, don't forget".

I was assigned to South Melbourne police station. Before starting all graduates had a two week vacation. The five girls from our squad booked a group holiday to Great Keppel Island - *camping*.

All the girls, except me, brought appropriate camping items. I brought lots of clothes! The other girls all thought this was hilarious.

We had a lot of fun, drinking, sun baking, swimming and partying with the other tourists - some from all over the world. I don't remember kissing anyone, probably because I was being faithful to surfer cop. What a waste! But at least two of the other girls were making the most of it. There was a proportionally larger number of young men, all with hot bods and suntans, on the island.

One night we had all gone to sleep quite late and inebriated, when we were all woken up by strange animal noises that seemed to be getting closer and closer.

It was pretty funny that we had just graduated as fully fledged cops (about to protect society against all sorts of ills!) But at least two of us were petrified. It was even funnier when we found out it was possums grabbing some of our left out camp food and fighting over it.

Not long after graduating I broke up with the surfer dude. It was a short lived romance.

Chapter 3

Charles "The Sexy Saint" My First True Love

I was twenty years old and fresh out of the Police Academy when I met Charlie, the football star of his local club. Charlie was also a chef. A very sexy combination. I fell in love pretty quickly.

The first time he stayed over, I woke up the next morning to hear noises coming from my kitchen. Upon entry I found this blonde, bronzed, 6'2" young man, whistling away, wearing only his jeans, six pack exposed, making me breakfast.

I was hooked. Our romance was blissful. He was the hero of the local football club. Everyone loved him. In later years I would describe him as a real man who wasn't afraid to show his sensitive side.

What was wrong with me? Why did I ever let this kind hearted beautiful man, who absolutely loved and adored me, go? (More about this later).

Charlie left little presents at my doorstep. I would get home from work and find a poem in a coffee mug, or a cake. We were in love and inseparable. He was a "Saint" literally, and played Australian Rules Football for "The Saints".

His mother was dying of Motor Neuron disease, horrible and debilitating. You are trapped in your own body and eventually lose all your functions, but here's the kicker, your brain is still active!

Charlie's father had died years before, a mean angry drunk who used to beat Charlie and his brothers. Charlie is one of five children. His oldest brother, got it the worst. His younger brother escaped most of it. Charlie nursed his mum, a lovely woman who attempted to keep her sense of humor despite the horrible disease.

Charlie kept the family together, his two younger sisters and his younger brother were at home, so he played father figure to them also. Money was tight but he always had a smile on his face and a healthy sense of humor.

Charlie took pleasure in whipping up exotic tasting meals from items like "Spam". Everything he cooked was delicious!

Meeting Charles

My girlfriends and I went to one of the hottest nightclubs at the time - Chevron, on St.Kilda Road.

There was a large line to get in but I knew one of the bouncers, plus my girlfriends and I normally entered via the VIP section. As we were all young, hot, fun and fashionable.

The place was pumping. Great music and the dance floor was full. We found a spot and danced together, probably intimidating for any guy to approach us. I noticed a bronzed blonde, 6'2", beautifully-proportioned young man moving slowly towards me. We locked eyes and he smiled in a way that melted all my inhibitions away.

"Hi, I'm Charlie and what's your name, beautiful?"

I can't remember all we said to each other that night. The music was loud, the dance floor was hot and I knew I wanted him immediately. I found out that Charlie had just got back from working on Great Keppel Island as a chef. Meant to be!

We swapped stories about the island and Charlie said he "wished he had met me there" but he had a girlfriend back then, anyway... but they had just broken up. So sad, not. Charlie asked for my number and of course I gave it to him without hesitation.

One of our first dates was a get-together at Charlie's local football club. It was obvious Charlie was the star of the club. When we walked into the room everyone wanted a piece of him and I loved that I was there with him. It made him even hotter to me. I wanted him more because everyone else did too.

Charlie moved easily through the world. He was comfortable in his own skin and present and kind to everyone and at the same time a real man. He had a positive attitude, despite dealing with a difficult home situation.

The first time we made love, he was gentle and kissed me all over, telling me how beautiful my body was and making me feel like I was going to explode with ecstasy. We were both inexperienced lovers but enjoyed the mutual discovering of sexual experiences. We were so in love it was blissful. We practiced a lot, fucking like rabbits every chance we got.

I don't ever remember my mother giving me the sex talk. In fact, my younger sister got her period before me and she instructed me on what I should do in that area. When I started using tampons I thought, "It's hard enough getting that up there how will a man's penis ever fit?" We had sex education class in school and the only thing I can remember is that an elephant's gestation period is almost two years.

Over the years I have experienced a range of shapes and sizes in the penis department. And just as the sexually evolved "Samantha" in a "Sex and The City" episode complained (to her girlfriends' surprise), "He's too big", there is such a thing as too large. And, the reverse is true too. Yes it can be too small.

Generally though, my girlfriends and I agree, it's more about what you do with it than the overall measurements. For me, and all the women I know, foreplay starts for us BEFORE we get into the bedroom - the romancing and flirting and anticipation gets me wet.

That's why for me, generally, if I really like someone I don't jump into bed with them immediately. Once you have made love for the first time, there will never be another *first* time with that man *ever* again.

I love the build-up. The wanting him so much that I almost give in... And the next time we meet we are ready to tear each other's clothes off. It's all we have been thinking about.

Long Distance Love - Does the Heart Grow Fonder?

The first crack in our armor came when Charlie got offered a contract to play football for a team on the opposite side of the country. A five hour and at the time, very expensive flight away.

Of course, Charlie wanted me to come with him but I was at the beginning of my police career. I had just spent nine months training in the Academy after which you do another eighteen months on-the-job training before you become a fully fledged cop.

I went to visit him. Leaving him at the airport, I was sobbing and he was crying too. I almost could not get on the plane but we agreed we would do the long distance thing for now until we could work something out.

Peter

I couldn't help it, the resentment that Charlie had 'left me behind' crept in. I was also young and had a pretty high libido, and I was getting a lot of attention, particularly from a guy I had met through my girlfriends.

Peter had been flirting with me, he was tall, hot and had a successful business and fancy car. I was feeling lonely.

In a moment of weakness I agreed to go on a date. After all I was 21 and my boyfriend was a thousand miles away. One date wouldn't hurt. One date turned into two, then just one kiss wouldn't hurt and then my raging hormones would not sleep.

Finally, after a heavy foreplay session in his car when he was dropping me home one night I couldn't take it anymore and invited Peter inside.

We kissed passionately. I could feel a tingling sensation all through my body as he kissed my lips, my neck and back to my lips with increasing heat. I led him to my bedroom and he gently placed me down on the bed.

He straddled me with his strong legs and slowly lifted up my top. He then lifted his shirt over his neck and threw it on the bed beside us, exposing his tanned, broad, smooth chest and strong biceps.

I moved my hands all over his glistening chest as he began kissing my neck again, right near my ear, my weak spot, I was wet with anticipation. I pulled him towards me and felt beautiful skin on skin as I fumbled with undoing the top button of his jeans. I could feel his hard, big, dick inside his jeans as he brushed against me. I couldn't stand it any longer and neither could he as I helped him pull down my jeans. We were both panting heavily.

He was about to enter me when the hallway phone began to ring. I attempted to drown the sound out as I pulled him in to me. The answering machine clicked on "Hey babe, it's late, I thought you would be home. God I miss you. I wish I was with you now. I love you..."

I pushed Peter off me. "I'm sorry you have to go." Peter stared back at me in dumbfounded shock, his rock hard dick half out of his pants. "I'm sorry... I can't do this". Poor Peter.

I was strong for a couple of weeks but Peter, surprisingly, kept calling me and I almost relented. Fortunately a girlfriend of mine made me promise not to ruin the surprise but she informed me that Charlie was coming home to surprise me. Luckily, otherwise I would have been busted!

Chapter 4

Charlie Returns, The Spell Is Broken and Joe the Vice Cop

Charlie 'surprised me' with his return. He showered me with love and vowed he had missed me so much. I was so happy to have him home and for a short while it was blissful. But I also knew he had mainly come back because his mother was getting much worse and he was needed here to help. Of course this was admirable but I couldn't shake the feelings of resentment that he had left me in the first place and thought it was 'really his fault' that I had been 'talking to' other guys.

Joe the Vice Cop

While Charlie was away I had also been flirting with a vice cop who I met during training at the Police Academy gym. I kept bumping into him at the Underground Nightclub. Why did I keep bumping into him? Why was I getting tempted?

One night Charlie and I had a big fight, I can't remember what about but I was angry and I finally agreed to go on a date with Joe, the vice cop, just to see how I felt. I was beginning to question my love for Charlie.

Joe picked me up and we went to the movies. The whole time I regretted it, feeling so guilty and realizing I was in love with Charlie. What an idiot I was to jeopardize what I had with him. Okay, no harm, Charlie will never find out, I didn't really do anything anyway except go to the movies, I didn't even properly kiss him and now I know for sure, I LOVE CHARLIE! I love him so much. Phew.

I called Charlie the next morning to apologize for our stupid fight and to tell him that I loved him. He was acting a little weird. I thought he would be as ecstatic as I was to hear those 'three little words' and me apologizing for anything in those days was pretty rare!

Charlie said, almost too casually, "Where were you last night?"

I gulped and then, quick thinking, "I called in to see my mum". I started to feel nervous.

"Why don't you tell me the truth?" He said.

I panicked "What are you talking about? I am. Are you calling me a liar?" Now, I was really backing myself into a corner.

Charlie proceeded to tell me that he came over last night to apologize to *me* and brought some flowers. He saw me getting out of another man's car. Oh Fuck!

"Charlie, listen we had a fight, I was angry, I just went to the movies with one of my cop friends. Nothing happened, we are just friends."

"Why were you wearing your sexy underwear?" He said.

"What are you talking about?".

"Yeah, I waited until you went inside and then I watched you through the window."

"What? That is just creepy, that is so wrong."

"I know, but I couldn't help it, I wanted to see your face, see if I could find out if you were playing up on me and you are!".

"I'm not. Okay, look I went on a date with him because I was angry with you but the good news is that I realized through the whole date how much I love you. I felt so guilty. I'm sorry, can we just forget about it? I love you, I won't ever do that again. I'm sorry." I said.

Charlie' whole demeanor changed. I had never seen him look like this before. He looked as if I had stabbed him in the heart.

Charlie Returns, The Spell Is Broken and Joe the Vice Cop

"You were my princess, in a million years I never thought you would betray me. I can't trust you now. It's over!" He said.

"Nooo!" I cried. Then he hung up on me.

Chapter 5

Loss of Love and Innocence A Broken Heart

I was inconsolable. My girlfriends tried to help but there was nothing they could do. My heart was broken and I couldn't take it back. My friend, Linda, suggested to write him a letter.

I did and I went around to his house to give it to him. Charlie was walking down his driveway towards the front gate.

Before I could give him the letter he yelled at me. "Get away from me you whore." Sometime later I got angry, I mean, come on? I didn't even kiss the guy properly. But at the time I was devastated and felt guilty. I pleaded with him, sobbing and calling out "Please forgive me".

Charlie, the warm, sensitive, sexy loving man, was like a stone statue, cold and strong. "Get away from me. IT'S OVER!". He then proceeded to get in his car and drive off, leaving me sobbing on the nature strip.

Bandaids on a Broken Heart

A couple of weeks later my girlfriends' forced me to go out with them. Under duress I agreed after much force, "C'mon you can't sit around here another night feeling sorry for yourself. You have to come. At least drown your sorrows with us. Come for a couple of drinks and some good music."

Reluctantly I agreed and we went to Frank's Nightclub where I basically moped the whole time and thought my life was over.

I arrived home to find a letter under my door from Charlie. The gist of it was, "I came to see you because Linda said you were a mess and so upset, but you're out on a Saturday night partying! Obviously not that upset".

I called him immediately and left a message on his phone. "Charlie, Linda dragged me out and I was miserable, I didn't want to go. I wish I hadn't gone. Please call me." Another week of silence went by and then I began to get a little angry, I mean I didn't do anything that bad!

Chapter 6

My First Week on the Job and First Punch In the Face

I was twenty years old and full of excitement as I arrived at South Melbourne police station for the tour of my first training station. I was greeted by the 'local mentally unstable but harmless man', who every morning when the Constable on duty that day went out front to raise the flag, he would wait for the occasion, salute, and then be on his way.

From the outside the police station looked very nice, bright fresh white paint, a two story spanish mission looking building with a pretty little garden, green lawn and flagpole out front.

Not so nice on the inside. I was shown around. At 'the watch house', where prisoners were entered into 'the watch house book', I noticed dried splattered blood on the pages.

There were two holding cells, stark concrete, heavy bars, two iron beds with thin mattresses, folded heavy grey blanket and thin pillow on each. A dull silver toilet base in the back with a roll of toilet paper sitting below on the floor. No privacy.

It began to sink in, what I had actually signed up to do and I had to give myself 'a good internal talking to'.

"What did you think it was going to be like? This is the real deal, so you better get on with it."

Our first afternoon shift I was on the Divisional van with a Senior Constable and our first order of the day was to serve a warrant for arrest in the local high rise commission flats (social welfare housing).

My First Week on the Job …

As we pulled up to the high rise low income buildings, the SC said , "Never park in the driveway."

"Why not?" I asked.

He said, "We will get pelted with pot plants and whatever else they can throw down on us and also wear your hat in the elevator."

"Why?" I asked.

"Because when they see us coming they put spit on the inside roof of it to fall on our heads." This location I ended up visiting many times for various reasons, calls to domestics, more warrant serving etc.

I also worked with a cop who immigrated from Sri Lanka with his family. He looked more like a hot male model from GQ Magazine than a cop.

We became good friends, and once when driving past this building he said, "That's where I first lived with my family when I came to Australia".

I had only been out of the Academy a few weeks when I got my first punch in the face and it was by a woman!

It was Melbourne Cup day, the horse race that "stops the nation" and a public holiday. Even if you don't bet on the horses normally, most people are in some sort of office sweep for this race.

I had just started day shift and it was only 10am when we got a call to go to one of the local pubs to assist with a drunken woman customer.

On the way to the pub, the Senior Constable driving informed me that "Women drunks are the worst". I should have paid more attention.

Upon arrival at the local pub the Bar Manager pointed out to a woman, in her 50's, teetering on a bar stool, a bag of groceries at her feet.

"She's wet herself too."

My partner, nodded and muttered "charming" as we approached her. He seemed to know who she was and said to the disheveled woman with a beehive hair do and lipstick smudged above her top lip, "C'mon Annie, you're starting a bit early today!"

As we helped, Annie out of the pub and into the divisional van she slurred at us, "Mee Grocereezz". I retrieved them for her, broken eggs and all and popped them in the van too.

When we arrived back at the station I stood by her helping her to stand as the watch house sergeant entered her details in the watch house book saying, "You can just sleep it off here for a few hours and you will be as good as gold."

Then to me said "Search her pockets." As I motioned to do so, Annie pulled away from me, clenched her fist and punched me full force in the cheek. I reeled backwards into the wall and think I actually saw stars like in a TV cartoon.

Annie ended up being my first court case also. She was charged with 'assaulting a police officer' and it turns out she was one of the oldest prostitutes in town and she had about fifteen pages of prior convictions.

The day I went to court as I got up and began to give my 'evidence' as to what occurred, she had a huge fake coughing fit and the judge had to call a short recess.

When Annie finally got up to give her story she told the judge that I stole $50 from her and that she only 'accidentally brushed my cheek'. I was furious and mortified at her blatant lies but all the other cops in court that day thought it was hilarious free entertainment.

It was a great lesson to learn though, before that I thought women didn't punch people, but from that day on I was very wary and managed to avoid getting punched again.

A Few Firsts...

I had been stationed at my new training station, South Melbourne, for a few weeks and was settling in quite well.

Sergeant Robinson was a jovial cop, with a friendly face, slightly greying hair, a small mustache and the worst cop humor! He been around for a while, seen a lot and took great pleasure in 'educating' me with a lot of firsts, he felt it was his duty. For example; I was on day shift, at the front desk one day when he popped his head around the corner and asked, "Hey, Constable Wilkins, have you ever seen a dead body?" Even though I protested that I had in fact seen a dead body at the Morgue during my training, he scoffed and said, "No a real one, on the streets!" He said "Come on, let's go!" He left one of the other constables in charge of the front desk and off we went to a local boarding house.

The dead body he had been referring to was a man who had died in this Boarding house a few days before and he was only discovered because of the smell coming from his room. It was the middle of summer and I learned that a body, left like this for a few days, bloats and begins to move because of the maggots taking up residence on his person.

It was a shocking sight to see. The Coroner began to prepare taking the body out. Other cops and detectives searched the small, cheap, sad room while I attempted not to throw up and remain looking professional. One of the cops said "Hey Sarge, check this out." He proceeded to open a small letter envelope and show us the contents inside. He poured into his hand, and we observed, various-sized loose diamonds. "Do you think they're real?" He asked the Sarge, who answered, "Probably. I could use one of those for the wife, that would make her real happy." He winked at me and then said "Make sure you don't lose any of those. I'm sure there is a record somewhere of how many this poor old soul had on his possession and tempting as it might be to slip one in your pocket, we must be held to a higher standard. Besides you will never sleep well again if you do this."

On the way back to the station we stopped off to get a bag of the very popular South Melbourne Market

My First Week on the Job ...

dim sims. Each one the size of your hand. I was not able to eat one that day, or ever again, as it somehow reminded me of the bloated yellowing- brown, moving, dead body of that man.

One night shift the sarge asked me if "I had ever been to a Brothel?" "Ah, no." I said. So we stopped outside a cute- looking house with no sign except for a red lamp light. Sarge buzzed the buzzer and we were let in to a foyer by a lady who seemed to know the Sarge well. He introduced me as "one of the new trainees" and said, "Go say hi to the girls".

He directed me to a small side room with a sliding door that was half open and a few girls, that looked around my age, (early twenties), were sitting on a large L-shaped sofa, flicking through magazines, knitting or watching the tv that was on in the corner. All were dressed in lingerie with loose gowns half open. They all looked pretty bored and barely acknowledged my presence as I nervously said "Hi" shuffling uncomfortably on my feet. The Sarge then called over to me and gave me a quick tour of the house. A few bedrooms simply set up with a bed, wash basin, some towels and side table with lamp and tissues and condoms. The last room of the house, the Sarge opened the closed door and chuckled at my shocked look when he said "This one's the dungeon". There was no bed, the walls were painted black, the lighting was low, and there was a bench in the middle of the room with some whips and chains on top. "For the naughty boys", My sarge said.

As we drove away, he said, "Your first brothel, what did you think?" I said "It seemed sad." The Sarge nodded, "Yeah but it's better than them being on the streets, provides a service, all kinds out there."

My First Week on the Job …

Meeting One of Australia's Most Notorious Criminals.

I was on duty one day at the St. Kilda Police front desk when a heavily tattooed man wearing a 'wife beater' shirt and a handle-bar mustache, entered.

"Hey Luv, I'm here to report on bail".

Newly-released criminals on bail were required to report to their local police station once a week to sign the bail book. Once he had signed the book and was about to leave he said "You are pretty cute Luv, how about a date?".

I replied, "It's Constable Wilkins and No thanks."

I inquired later to my Sergeant, "What was Mark Reid in prison for?" My Sergeant chuckled and replied "Chopper? Armed robbery, assault, and allegedly a few gangland murders."

Years later when Eric Banna portrayed him in the movie, I thought he did a good job.

Chapter 7

Cops and Prostitutes

We were driving down a dimly lit street, my first night shift at St. Kilda Police station. I said to my partner (as I noticed two very tall women wearing glittery outfits and wigs). "They must be going to a fancy dress".

My partner rolled his eyes at me and as we got closer, he rolled down his drivers side window to address them. I noticed that they were not women at all but men wearing makeup and dressed like ladies. It was the first time I had ever seen a transvestite and a prostitute as well.

"Hello Officer" said one of them as they leaned seductively in and smiled out me. "Who's the cutie pie?". "Our newest trainee", replied my partner.

I got to know the local street pros quite well. Most of them were heroin addicts just trying to pay for their next fix which they needed to be able to stomach doing the work they did. There were no fantasy-type women like portrayed in "Pretty Women". These were poor souls, just barely making it through life and the trannies were mostly doing it to pay for their hormone replacements and saving up for the sex change.

I met "Robyn Reed" when my sergeant played a trick on me at the station. He called me from the watch house front desk one night and asked me to do a strip search of a female suspect they brought in.

The rules at St. Kilda police station were female cops searched females and male cops searched the males. We did full strip searches in St. Kilda as there were a lot of drugs etc.

Cops & Prostitutes

I entered the room to see a tall prostitute with bright red lips, blonde hair, short skirt and large pointy breasts. She had very long bright painted red chipped fingernails which she was tapping on the desk.

"Hello Robyn" I said, "Do you have anything on your person I should be worried about? No needles or anything like that right?"

Robyn smiled sweetly and seductively at me as I put my gloves on and replied in a deep husky voice "No Officer".

As I instructed her to begin to take off her top etc. I noticed she had a rather large Adam's apple and big hands. I began to suspect and said, "Robyn, have you had the operation?"

"No love that's why I am doing this to pay for getting the chop. Though the hormones are working well, check out these, pretty good yes?" Robyn lifted up her top to expose her pointy breasts.

At the same time I noticed some "bobbing heads " outside the window. My Sarge and the night shift crew were waiting to see my shock as I discovered Robyn was a "he".

"Wait here." I said. I left the room and found the Sarge sitting "innocently" reading the newspaper in the lunch mess room and said to him, "Sarge, Robyn is a 'he'. I can't search 'her'."

Most of the time we left the street prostitutes alone to do their thing, but every few months we would do what's called "a clean up operation".

Myself and another policewoman had to dress like we were prostitutes. My Sarge said, "Not like in Pretty Woman, dress like you haven't had a shower for a week, dirty hair, etc."

My partner would hide in the bushes and I would have to get the "John" to say what he wanted sexually and for how much and then we would arrest him for 'soliciting for prostitution'.

Most of them would get a fine and a scare but it was also potentially very dangerous as one policewoman got run over when the "John" drove off and another had just done an armed robbery and we almost got shot.

I remember one man, as soon as I pulled out my badge he said "Oh no I've never done this before. I just had a fight with my fiancé and I was walking along and saw you and thought you looked cute and maybe this would help me feel better."

A couple of months later I got a call at the station. A woman on the phone said "Hello Constable you don't know me but you arrested my fiancé not long ago for soliciting for prostitution. I was wondering if you think I should still marry him? ".

I was thinking NO! But I said, "I do remember that he told me it was his first time so it was lucky that we stopped him because most of the prostitutes on the street are addicts and can be dangerous. I'm sorry I can't really give you advice on this matter".

Male Prostitutes

When I was a young cop 'AIDS' was a scary, life threatening disease that "everyone knew you could get from sharing a needle or having unprotected sex and was prevalent with homosexuals." That's about all we knew. There was a number of people using "it" as a weapon. Robberies with criminals brandishing an "aids infected syringe" as their weapon of choice.

There was one particular young male prostitute going around town saying he was "taking pleasure in spreading it". We spent a few shifts looking out for this person.

The 'pick up' spot of choice was the car park adjacent to Luna Park and I remember one night an expensive looking Jag pulling up. Just as a young male prostitute hopped into his car, we approached. Upon checking the upmarket well dressed middle aged businessman's credentials it was established that he was married to a woman, had two young children and lived in an affluent suburb of Melbourne.

We let the businessman go with a warning to "at the very least use protection," telling him of the possible dangers of this particular street prostitute and to be honest with his wife and also reminding him we had his details on police file now re the warning 'soliciting for prostitution'.

The young male prostitute in question, it turned out, did not have AIDS but was loving the drama of it all.

Night shifts are a consecutive week of working nights, commencing 11pm until 7am every day until the 7th day, usually a Sunday, and you come back to work that same afternoon and work the 3-11 afternoon shift which is called 'a quick change over'. Then you have a few days off.

It is tradition that the night shift will have a night shift barbecue before the few days off to celebrate the end of the night shift and have drinks together and sometimes actually a real barbecue. They ranged from small little get togethers to huge parties.

The local pubs would often supply the beer for free to us as a thank you for keeping the streets clean and dealing with their drunks!

One night shift got out of control in the Cattani Gardens. A group of cops gathered in the huge park adjacent to the boardwalk foreshore.

I left when I noticed some of the local prostitutes arriving and a couple of cops actually making out with them. A few prostitutes over the years have confided in me about a couple of particular cops at my station that would exchange sexual favors for various misdemeanors. This was few and far between but I was shocked and disgusted by this. Using the power we had to protect and serve, this was totally unacceptable but I was too young to know how to deal with this knowledge and being a whistleblower is dangerous as a young cop.

Thankfully I had left this particular night, as soon after, the interstate detectives who were in town, joined the party and began shooting their firearms off. One bullet went across the road into a high rise apartment where an elderly man, getting up in the middle of the night to go to the bathroom had a bullet fly right past his nose, missing him by inches, landing in his bathroom wall.

There were some major suspensions with locals cops after this incident, obviously.

We arrested Robyn Reed again a few weeks later after a man came into the station reporting he had been robbed.

A welldressed man recounted his story that he had picked up a prostitute, he described Robyn to a tee. She had directed him to drive down a lane way and park. Just as he pulled out his dick to get it sucked, two young men stood over him, one had a tomahawk and said "Give us your watch and all your money or we will chop it off." "Of course I gave them my Rolex and my wallet. My father gave me that watch", he said.

This little armed robbery situation had been going on for a while but most of the victims didn't report it because they didn't want to admit they had been with a street prostitute.

Robyn was charged with five counts of armed robbery and so were her accomplices. I felt a little sorry for Robyn the day I went to serve some more counts of armed robbery on her while she waited on remand at Pentridge Prison. She had not had 'the operation' yet so she was 'processed' as a man. Robyn still had the boobs though and because she was no longer getting the hormones, behind bars, she had quite a growth of stubble.

The Day I Delivered Warrants at Pentridge Prison

I arrived at the front reception area and explained I was here to serve more warrants (charges) on a prisoner, Robyn Reed.

The prison receptionist asked me to hand over my firearm, signed it into the book and then pointed through a window to a secure building across the enclosed prison grounds, with some garden area, where a number of prisoners were wandering around, sweeping paths, others sitting on benches.

He said "Just go through there and buzz the buzzer at the front of that building and a guard will let you in."

I gulped in shock as I replied, "You expect me to walk through there in my police uniform past all those prisoners by myself?"

He replied, "Don't worry, that's the low security section, minor offenses."

As I walked slowly across the grounds, my heart beating hard against my chest, feigning confidence amongst wolf whistles and sniggers I suddenly hear, "Wendy?"

"Oh shit!", I think it's someone I've arrested, that knows my first name!

Before I could recover, one of Charlie' footballer mates approached me and said, "What are you doing here?"

I said, "What are you doing here?"

He replied he had a second drink driving charge and had to serve six months. He let me know that it wasn't as bad as he thought as they were separated from the hard core criminals and he was about to get out in the next month after only one month inside, for good behavior.

He introduced me to a few of his 'prison mates' and when one of them inquired if I was single, he warned him that I was his friend's girlfriend so he better "back off".

Chapter 8

Cops and Guns

Our training for using our standard police issue Smith and Wesson 38's was pretty basic when I joined the police force.

In the Academy we were taught how to shoot. This was my very first time using a firearm and I remember being surprised at the "kick back" as my very first bullet landed in the police academy firing range ceiling!

The basics I learned, were you have to 'cock the gun' and get a sight line for any kind of possible aim of accuracy. This basic training frankly 'goes out the window' when you are using it in self defense in the heat of the moment with all the tension and adrenaline running through your veins. We were put through basic training, an obstacle course of sorts, with different scenarios and civilians popping up in the middle of armed assailants and then our shots would be added up, including how many civilian injuries and deaths we caused.

Later when I took 'The Police Pursuit Driving Course', 'witches hats' were placed along the course. If you hit any, it meant you killed innocent pedestrians. I only hit two.

Once out of the Academy, every six months you had to "requalify' by going to the shooting range and getting 36 out of 40 rounds on a target body silhouette or you were not licensed to carry a firearm. Every time I went to qualify my partner at the time would joke "how many do you want us to get on yours for you?"

I was not an accurate shot and I did not and still don't like firearms but there was "no way" I would be on the streets as a cop without one and despite the joking around about accuracy etc, I did not know one cop in my five years on the force who was "trigger happy".

I only had to draw my weapon a few times and thankfully never pulled the trigger but I did come very close one night.

It was soon after the Walsh street killings. Every cop was on edge and so upset because of the ambush and shooting of two young cops who were a few squads junior to me in the Academy. I knew them to say "hi" to. They were both based at our neighboring police station so we crossed paths regularly.

Constables Steven Tynan, 22, and Damian Eyre, 20 were checking reports of a suspect vehicle in Walsh Street, South Yarra, early hours of a quiet morning. The car had been left with the motor running in the middle of a suburban street and when the young trainee constables went to investigate they were both shot at point blank range, for no reason except that these particular criminals hated cops.

Steve and Damian had no chance and it was only then I realized for the first time that wearing a uniform and driving a police car we are walking, moving targets and these criminals see us before we see them.

I was on night shift the week after and my partner had been first on the scene after the murders of Steve and Damien. Constable Thomas and I were called to a suspect vehicle and both of us began to feel anxious, especially as 'Thomas' described to me in detail the carnage he witnessed on arrival at the young Constables' murder scene.

He said "They were gunned down without a chance".

The suspect vehicle turned out to be routine but later that night cruising down a dark alley 'known for prostitutes and crooks hanging out' we noticed a vehicle stationary with it's motor running and headlights on. We approached slowly in the divisional van and when we were about 20 feet away stopped and called out on our loud speaker. "Step out of the vehicle"

Cops & Guns

It was difficult to see as we were blinded by the car's headlights directly shining into ours. We could just make out a large figure behind the wheel. After some time the figure did not get out so again we called over the speaker. Nothing again.

This back and forth went on for sometime, eventually with more aggression on our part "SIR, TURN THE ENGINE OFF AND GET OUT OF THE VEHICLE. PUT YOUR HANDS WHERE WE CAN SEE THEM". Still Nothing.

Eventually we were out of our vehicle with our firearms drawn when slowly the man got out. He was large and over six foot tall.

"Put your hands up where we can see them".

Again, nothing. This went on it seemed like an eternity. I had my firearm drawn on him and attempting not to shake, nervously. He then reached across his jacket pocket and inside his jacket and I was sure he was going to pull out a gun and fire on us.

It was a split second before I almost pulled the trigger. Fortunately I didn't because he did not have a gun but I can understand the feeling of 'Shoot or be shot', as I truly believed he was going to shoot me at that moment and only a split second of hesitation made all the difference.

Fatal Shooting

Two weeks later my close friend and roommate from the Academy, (a truly wonderful policewoman, firm, fair, brave, smart and funny) accidentally shot and killed her partner in a police raid.

Sarah was on night shift. They attended a suburban house in their area in the early hours of the morning with several other cops. A known violent criminal was wanted on various serious charges and was believed to be staying there. As the police raided the front of the house, the man raced out the back sliding door with a rifle.

He pointed it straight at Sarah, who had her gun drawn on him and yelled. "Stop or I'll shoot". He aimed the rifle directly at Sarah and she thought he was going to shoot her so she pulled her trigger in self defense in a split second. At the same time her partner came from the other corner of the yard from behind the shadows and attempted to disarm the criminal by grabbing the man's rifle.

Unfortunately as her partner grabbed for the man and his rifle, Sarah's bullet missed the criminal and hit her partner straight to his head. Sarah had accidentally fatally shot her partner, instead of the criminal, when her partner got between him and her bullet.

Everything happened so quickly Sarah recounted to a few close colleagues later that she thought her partner had been shot by the criminal's rifle and did not realize it was her own bullet until sometime later.

It was later established that the rifle the criminal pointed at Sarah and squeezed on the trigger, was not loaded. Sarah had to live with this tragedy for the rest of her life. This horrible accidental shooting. The internal investigations department investigated and ruled that her partner technically did not follow protocol, when he came out of the shadows to disarm the man, but this was not any comfort at all of course to Sarah. She lost her young partner and friend and his wife became a young widow when he tragically lost his life on duty.

Working for The Chief Commissioner - Or I'm Not a Bloody Secretary

Around this time I was 'seconded' temporarily to work at the Police Commissioner's office for one month. I was furious. It was basically a glorified receptionist role and I wanted to be 'out on the streets'. I didn't join the police force to be a bloody receptionist!

My job consisted of going through the newspapers that landed on my desk every day and cutting out any 'police related articles' and fielding calls to the Chief Commissioner.

A large number of the calls revolved around frivolous police complaints such as, "How come the police get free McDonalds? I want to make a complaint about this!"

Side note: At the time I played on a Netball team with the Marketing Manager of McDonalds Victoria and she told me that the new Police Commissioner contacted McDonalds and said "Please don't give our Police free McDonalds we don't want to be seen as taking things for free."

McDonalds reps answered "that it was their prerogative and would continue to do this as their policy as they wanted to support the cops and the more police presence, the better for them".

Another complaint was a call, "I saw a uniformed cop park at our local supermarket in a police car and then buying groceries, is that what our taxpayers money is going to? He should buy his groceries on his own time!"

My answer "Ma'am the local police stations that have jail cells get the Watch house officer to buy groceries for our prisoners such as bread and milk etc and fruit."

And another phone call, "I saw two cops park at a No standing zone. Why didn't they get a ticket? Why can they just park anywhere they want?"

My answer "Perhaps they were going to save a person being raped or murdered and by the time they found a legal parking spot it might be too late!"

I continually called my Sergeant at Russell Street Police Station asking "Sir, when can I report back to normal duties?"

His answer, "It's an honor to work for the Chief Commissioner, soon, it's just temporary."

One day the Police Commissioner called me into his office and began a discussion about whether a trainee cop should carry a gun. He did not know that Sarah was one of my close friends. He said if a trainee didn't carry one then the tragedy of the accidental shooting death of the young Constable would not have occurred. I disagreed with this thinking and told him so.

I said " Sir, the man pointed a rifle straight at a cop, it has to be assumed it was loaded. There is no time when someone is squeezing a trigger and pointing a rifle straight at you and that must be considered as life threatening and you must defend yourself. If the rifle was loaded and the trainee wasn't armed the trainee could have been killed. Also as trainees we are out on the streets doing all the duties of fully fledged cops and the public doesn't know we are a trainee. I don't think Sarah would have acted any differently if she had been on the force for ten years."

Apart from this disagreement, I had a lot of respect for him and thought he was a great Chief Commissioner. The fact that he entertained such discussions and sought the opinions of a new trainee, such as myself, was impressive. I was sad to see him retire many years later.

A couple of weeks later I was back to normal police duties on the streets and putting up with some of my colleagues jibs such as "how was your cushy "Sexetary job?".

Chapter 9

Crush on the Detective

David was in the SOG, which is the 'Special Operations Group' or as most cops refer to it: 'The Sons of God', that is, the SWAT team. He looked so hot in his uniform.

We met in the Police Academy. He was respected by his squad mates. He had a degree and was a little older than most of us. He had an air of confidence that was very attractive. My favorite combination smart, good looking, great 'bod' and tall. He knew my boyfriend Charlie, through football. David played and also coached his local team.

When I first broke up with Charlie, I began to spend more time with David. I taught aerobics a couple of times a week in those days, in between shifts. I wore the leotards, "Jane-Fonda and Olivia-Newton-John style".

Once David asked me to take his footy team through an aerobics session to get them to start working on their flexibility.

Before I got up to take them through a session, there were quite a few wolf whistles and sniggers. David immediately made sure that they would all 'show me the utmost respect' and silenced them.

I began to develop a crush on him but David had a long term sweetheart he had met in high school so… I began to date a cocky young real estate agent.

Soon after, David broke up with his long time girlfriend and he asked me out on a date but timing is everything and I was starting to fall for the Real Estate Agent. By the time The Real Estate Agent and I broke up a year later, I had heard David had got back together with his ex.

Crush on the Detective

One night David called me and let me know he was in the city for a friend's wedding and "did I want to meet up at a city nightclub later, where they all were going?".

I thought "No, this is dangerous!"

I went to another party but I could not stop thinking about him. I got home early from the party and was about to take my makeup off when I thought "why not just go meet him? We can have a catch up at the nightclub and that's all, after all we are friends."

Then I thought to myself "Don't be silly it's nearly midnight "Go to bed!"

Then I thought "I'm wide awake, I could just go have one drink with him. It's getting late, If I can't find him at the nightclub I'll just come home".

As soon as I arrived I saw David and I knew I wanted him. A few drinks later, he convinced me to come and stay at his hotel.

"You can't drive, you've had too much to drink. I'll sleep on the floor and you can have the bed."

I was lying on the bed and David lay on the floor right beside me. After a few minutes of looking at the ceiling I leaned over the bed and said, "That floor does not look comfortable. You may as well sleep in the bed with me."

As soon as David got in the bed beside me I could not help myself and neither could he. I could feel every part of his strong muscled body so close to mine and his rock hard dick begging me to let him in. Every nerve ending throughout my body and his seemed to join together. I could not wait for him to enter me. The tension of months of skirting around each other exploded in ecstasy as my whole body shook in bliss.

Not too long after this he married his childhood sweetheart.

Chapter 10

Frank and Nightclub Fever

Anyone who was anyone in the scene in town hung out in the VIP section of my friend, Frank's nightclub. My girlfriends and I never bought a drink there, though we drank plenty in those days. Funnily enough neither did the movers and shakers, they were always looked after by the owners and promoters, only the poor plebs handed over their hard earned money across the bar.

Frank and I flirted with each other constantly.

Frank was hot, tall, smooth olive skin, melting smile and owner of the hottest nightclub in town. I had a huge crush on him which grew as I got to know him. He spoke with a soft, silky sensual voice and seduced me with his friendly ways.

He had also been in the Navy and one of our first conversations was about the pros of discipline that the Services and the Police Force had in common. We talked about having to shine our shoes in the "Academy". He had respect for me and my vocation.

One night it was getting late, my girlfriends were leaving and Frank said, "Stay for one more drink".

We ended up having a long chat about the merits of having such strong discipline training and how "everyone should do a stint in the service".

I was loving the attention from him and feeling buzzed from the alcohol. I mentioned something about maybe I shouldn't drive home just yet.

Frank and Nightclub Fever

Frank said "why don't you come back to my place next door for a little while."

I was shocked - he had a place next door. He informed me that he kept a small place for when he had a really late night so he didn't have to drive home.

It was a small hotel type room, studio apartment, modern and clean lines. One thing led to another and I stayed the night. I remember the room details more than any sex that night.

Years later comparing notes with one of my girlfriends she informed me she had spent the night there with him also!

Frank was so charming. He never came across as a sleaze bag. He was discreet and made you feel like you were special, also incredibly generous.

We only slept together twice over the years. We were never going to be a couple, just good friends that fucked a couple of times.

Frank entertained everyone who came to town at one time or another. A famous American singer came to town for a concert and developed a huge infatuation for a local actress/singer in a band and pursued her madly.

Frank and I were both discussing this and I said "I can't understand why he would go after another girl when he, at the time, was married to one of the most beautiful supermodels in the world."

Frank agreed, saying "Yeah he even wrote a song about her 'My ...... girl'".

He continued, "But you know what he said to me when I asked him the same question. 'Frank do you like mashed potatoes?'". Frank said he answered, "Yeah I do". The singer said, "So do I, but I don't want it every night."

Ever since then every time I hear this song I change the radio station.

Chapter 11

Charlie and I Reunite and My Boyfriend Gets Arrested

My girlfriends and I would often go to another hot spot in town called The Ritz nightclub. We, of course were friends with the Owners/Managers and treated like VIPS there also. Models, Footballers and the party people of Melbourne could be seen there regularly.

For a few Wednesday nights the Managers began a promotion that the person who brought the most friends to the club that night would win a $1000. My girlfriends and I knew a lot of people and we teamed up and won twice! I'm not sure that the head count was accurate but we weren't complaining of course.

One night I joined my girlfriends there a little late as I had just finished afternoon shift at St.St. Kilda Police station.

As soon as I arrived the girls informed me that Charlie was there with a girl! Not just a girl but a lingerie model/actress.

I felt my stomach turn and couldn't believe how jealous I felt. I gulped down a drink and then with as much confidence and cover I could muster, I graciously went up to them and said "Hi".

Charlie seemed surprised to see me, though I'm sure he knew this was *my* local hang out. I was very polite and then returned back to my girlfriends and we proceeded to swap stories about as much as we could about this girl. She had recently broken up with a well known footballer and apparently she was nice enough but not the smartest of girls.

I couldn't help it, as the night went on I became the greeneyed-monster and all I could think about was how much I wanted Charlie back.

I had parked my car a little down the street and so as I was about to leave I made my move. I went up to Charlie when the girl was not by his side and said "Do you mind walking me to my car, I don't want to go by myself. I know from work there has been a few rapes reported in the area and I'm feeling a little nervous.

I left out the part that the 'rape' that had been reported was by a local prostitute who reported one of her "Johns" who had pulled a knife on her and had not paid for services rendered. It was the second time it had happened to her. We found the guy, charged him, but unfortunately on the day of the court hearing our 'star' witness had just hit up with heroin before she got into the witness box.

Apart from the fact she could hardly stand up, she was not able to string more than a few words together so the case was dismissed.

Charlie walked me to my car and I couldn't help myself I immediately began interrogating him.

"How long have you been going out with her?"

Charlie said that "they were just friends and had been just hanging out".

"Well I miss you", I said and began to cry a little.

Charlie made sure I got into my car okay but he said "he missed me too and that he wanted to make sure his friend got home okay but could he come and see me tomorrow?"

I was so happy. Charlie and I got back together and things almost went back to normal for a while but I knew that I had pushed myself off that pedestal he had me sitting high on top of and I felt he didn't look at me quite the same way anymore - 'as his beautiful innocent princess who could do no wrong'. I also had little pangs of guilt that I knew deep down in my soul I had pushed that girl aside more out of jealousy than anything else.

I don't remember what Charlie and I had a fight about one day, but he drove home angry from my place and called me about half an hour later and said, "I think I'm in trouble".

He told me that he had punched a guy and he said the guy threatened him that he was going to be charged with assault. Charlie was not one to get into fights. He was tall and fit with huge arms but he was always the one talking his mates into keeping the peace. He won 'best and fairest' each year at his local footy club so this was a shock to me.

Apparently there had been some kind of minor road rage traffic altercation where the other driver had been cut off by Charlie driving and almost caused a car accident.

The guy stopped his car just ahead of Charlie, got out of his car and ran at Charlie with a metal pipe and Charlie just punched him once in self defense. I told Charlie to "go straight down to the police station and explain what happened, to get your side of the story in".

I spoke to the local police prosecutor who suggested Charlie should plead guilty.

I said, "No way he was just defending himself and the guy ran at him with a metal pipe".

The prosecutor explained that "they would go to court and see this older man against this 6'ft 2 young strong footballer who also had trained in boxing and there would be no way the jury would take his side." So Charlie ended up doing 12 months community service.

Some of the cops at my station took great pleasure in joking that I was consorting with a "criminal family". A few months earlier Charlie's younger brother was charged with growing marijuana plants in his back yard and was on probation for that too.

Chapter 12

Aliens and Cops Playing Pranks

When I worked at St. Kilda Station they were in the process of closing down some of the smaller area stations and combining them into one bigger station per area. Elwood police station was one of these.

During the transition and before permanent closure a St. Kilda cop would be rostered there for the day. If you had a ton of paperwork to catch up on it was the ideal place as it was quiet and rarely anyone would come in.

I volunteered and was half way through a non eventful day when I got a call. I answered, "Elwood Police Station". A frazzled voice on the other end said "Hello police? There is a robbery in progress at the Elwood Post office. A druggie is waving a needle around saying it's infected with AIDS and threating to stab anyone who comes close and asking everyone to hand over all their money and watches and stamps."

I quickly called St. Kilda Police station, and informed them I was closing up shop here and going to check it out and to send back-up."

A few minutes later I burst into the post office with my firearm drawn, scaring the shit out of the customers who were quietly going about their day buying stamps etc. There definitely had *not* been any "crazed druggie in there robbing the place."

After apologizing for scaring them all, I retreated, red faced.

Fuming, I called St. Kilda station and let them know I was not impressed and "I could have bloody shot

Aliens and Cops Playing Pranks

someone." Of course the culprits 'pleaded innocence' as to knowing anything about the event.

There was a couple of young cops that loved playing pranks at my station and one got so big it made the 6 o'clock news.

These cops burnt a large round circle on the grass at a foreshore car park. We had a local "mentally unstable but harmless guy", affectionately known as 'the Major' because he dressed in an army uniform (non issue) and would salute us all every time he entered the station.

The Major also had a photo ID card, he would produce with two different photos of himself, side by side, one wearing dark sunglasses and the other without.

The Major often hung around the station foyer, or he would come in and report sightings of various misdemeanors. Sometime we would give him tasks, such as "count all the red cars that passed a certain intersection between certain hours".

He would diligently report back with the numbers. The Major could come across as very credible if you met him once for a very short period and this one day these cops drove him down to the foreshore to show him this burnt ring.

They convinced him that he had seen a circular-type saucer flying across the sky coming from the direction of Frankston way, along the coast line and it landed in front of him here on the foreshore, for a few minutes and then took off again. These same cops had organized friends from Frankston area and along the foreshore to call the local news station with sightings. A news crew showed up and interviewed the Major as an eye witness to a UFO! I couldn't believe it made the 6.00pm news.

One hot summer evening there were two divisional vans operating and I was partnered on one with another female Senior Constable, Jenny. She was a great cop. Friendly, firm and fair. We got a call from the other van to meet us outside Luna Park for a possible job.

Aliens and Cops Playing Pranks

We pulled up beside the two male cops from our station, talking between cars and complaining about how hot it was and how many tourists were out and about.

One cop in the other van said, "Yeah you two ladies look like you need a cool down" then water bombed us right into the divisional van with two fully filled water balloons!

Jenny and I were soaked and before we had a chance to even respond, they drove off laughing their heads off. So, of course, we planned retaliation.

We bought some condoms at the local pharmacy and filled them up with water. Once armed, we went in hot pursuit all over Stkilda.

We gave chase following them up to the top of the Prince of Wales car park and finally had them cornered.

We jumped out of the van and got them good. We were hilariously satisfied but it didn't last long. Jenny had been driving and when she jumped out, in her haste, she had not put the hand brake on and the van was slowly moving towards the edge of the building. In horror, we raced towards it and she got there just in time to save the day. Phew that would have been difficult to explain.

I was driving the Inspector around one night shift and we passed by a minor car accident. Cops would rather not get involved in these minor issues, where there are no injuries as it's a ton of paperwork and "not real police work". Begrudgingly we stopped and checked out the situation, once all was clear we drove off.

The next night I gave my typed up report of the incident to the inspector to check over. As he read he began frowning and shaking his head.

I had written, "At approximately 11.30pm we were driving South along Fitzroy Street St. Kilda when I observed a minor traffic accident and asked Inspector Jones, "Should we stop, Sir, there's been an accident."

Inspector Jones replied "No bloody way let's get the fuck out of here before they see us." His frown turned to a chuckle as I gave him the actual correct report.

Chapter 13

My Girlfriend the Stripper... and Drugs

It was my friend, Valentina's hens night (Bachelorette party). We decided that we were going to go to a strip club after a few too many cosmopolitans.

There is a row of them in the city and we decided on, supposedly, the classiest one, 'The Men's Gallery'. As soon as we walked in I was confronted by one of my closest girlfriends, Linda, at the side of the stage, giving a spread eagled private dance to a customer. I saw, as they say, 'what she had for breakfast'! I certainly did not want to see her in that way, right up her vagina, but at the same time I was fascinated.

Watching the girls dance, the good ones with the fabulous bodies, is quite entertaining. Just as entertaining is the various men's reactions. Puppy dog types huffing and puffing and eager to rub their noses on the girls. Drunken boisterous wolf packs in suits out on the town for a good time without their wives. Whom they, incidentally, treat like ladies, while treating everyone else as whores. Sad, lonely strays that just want some kindness and company.

Linda was the youngest and first girl in our group to have her own business. She still is an excellent hairdresser and bought into a salon and was very successful. Linda met a boy, fell in love and together they had a lot of fun.

It was a time when Australia had one of the best dance party scenes, I think, in the world. (I have been to opening night parties in Ibiza at the renowned nightclubs, in New York and London. I have danced in front of world famous DJ's from Bali to Vegas to Thailand). It was the early days of ecstasy and DJ's making names for themselves.

My Girlfriend the Stripper…and Drugs

I've had some of the most fun in my life going to amazing dance parties, dancing all night with my friends on a half a pill. Back then if it was pure and clean all you wanted to do is dance and be happy and hug people, share the love. There is no way there would be aggression or fights and violence.

Unfortunately, some people would keep taking another and another pill and chasing that high, maybe for days and coming down with a thud. Also, you never know what the drug has been laced with, especially these days - much more dangerous.

Side story. We arrested a young girl for selling pills at a local nightclub. She was underage and while waiting for her legal guardian to arrive (before we could interview her) I made small talk with her while she kept rubbing her shoulder softly. I wasn't paying too much attention to this until her mother arrived and asked, "How's Henry?" The girl proceeded to take a pet rat called "Henry" out of his resting place upon her shoulder, under her jacket. I was mortified. I have a rat and mouse phobia.

Yes it might sound hypocritical that I indulged a little in illegal drugs also, cocaine and ecstasy every now and then. But the real criminals, I believe are the drug pushers.

I didn't think too much about it at the time but I do believe having this overall life experience made me a better cop. I never charged anyone for taking a drug, definitely not marijuana. Putting someone in jail for this, I think, is a real crime. What I was against was the seedy money-making, criminal side that pushes large quantities without regard for human life.

Fortunately I have a body system that won't ever allow me to over indulge, even after a few glasses of alcohol I throw up and get horrible hangovers so I don't over indulge. These days, I prefer a lovely dinner party with excellent company.

The most dangerous drug, when I was a cop, was heroin. Highly addictive. Heroin addicts that I met came from all walks of life and social standing. It did not discriminate. You could become an addict very quickly and spiral down fast. I would never try heroin. A vicious circle of chasing the high and eventually taking it just to not feel sick. Heroin addicts robbed their aging grandmothers and ruined families. Heroin addicts caused heartache to their loving parents, who, no matter how hard they tried to help their children watched helplessly on as their child destroyed their lives, living on the streets, prostituting themselves, debasing to the lowest form of human existence just to get their next hit.

Linda is a petite little girl with fabulous fashion sense and great dance skills, and she embraced these parties with gusto. Eventually she was taking a lot of drugs including cocaine. Linda is also bi-polar, and has a hard time saying "No". She would give away her drugs for free and people would take them.

Very soon she ended up selling her business, having no job and owing some dubious people over $10,000 - and being threatened daily. Nate, her boyfriend stuck by her. They had visited the strip clubs together several times before and Nate suggested maybe this was her way out, earn some quick money.

Linda told me the first time she danced she threw up afterwards, from nerves and shame, but after a while, getting to know the girls, she came to enjoy it.

Linda is self-deprecating and has a great sense of humor and she thought it was hilarious that she has walnut-sized boobs and was a stripper. Linda made good tips. She has the gift of the gab and is a good listener.

Linda told me she had a few regulars and they were very nice, just mostly lonely. Most of the time while Linda was dancing and flirting with the guys she was, at the same time, going over her shopping list in her head, "Milk, bread, maybe some chocolate."

Linda has great stories, including the famous married "action- hero" movie star with a thick accent who was visiting Australia. He took one of the girls back to his hotel for more than a dance. By the way, this is frowned upon by the clubs. Linda was very pragmatic and open about her job, well she had to be because half of the men she knew in Melbourne visited at one time or another. One night my boyfriend at the time, the real estate agent, called me from there. He was in the middle of a Bachelor party night. He put Linda on the phone and we all had a fun chat.

Linda confided in me that Valentina's husband, Vince, had been frequenting the strip club and had become obsessed with one of the girls. I didn't want to believe it. His wife, Valentina, is still a very good friend of mine, beautiful, intelligent, funny, a great mother, successful business owner and an amazing partner to him. Vince was also my friend.

There was no way I was going to tell my girlfriend unless there was absolute proof and I hoped it wasn't true.

Interestingly this girl, that Vince was apparently obsessing about, I had met a few months before. She was dating a real estate agent I knew, Matt, and he brought her to one of my parties.

Every Christmas eve I had a party in my loft and it was legendary fun. An eclectic group of friends coming together for lots of fabulous cocktails, fun conversations and dancing the night away. All the Christmas shopping had been done, work was over for a few days for most of us and it was almost the end of the year. And, it was summer. I look back on it, thinking I must have been the instigator of many very hungover Christmas lunches with family in my twenties.

Matt, my real estate friend, introduced her to me, a very pretty blonde with a great figure. One of my male friends at the party asked her, in general conversation, what she did for a living and she said she was a veterinary nurse. I was quite impressed with this as we all love animals and everyone was asking her lots of questions about it. I found out later that she made it all up to cover up her real job.

For some reason it really annoyed me that she was telling such a specific a lie. Matt told me her true vocation and that she had made this story up because there was "no way" he could tell his parents, and certain other people, that he was dating a stripper. Okay then, I thought, pretend you're a receptionist or a carer which are very admirable jobs, not a "years-of-university-study-to-get-qualified-in-helping-sick- injured-animals" veterinary nurse! That's not fair to the nurses that actually trained and studied for years.

My Girlfriend the Stripper…and Drugs

Before I had a chance to investigate the truth of the story about Vince, Matt contacted me and confirmed the story that his girlfriend was in fact being stalked by Vince. He asked me "because I knew Vince and his wife, and could I tell him to stop before he takes action, like letting Vince's wife know all about it". I felt like saying, "well that's what you get when you take your clothes off for a living for money to turn guys on." Though I stopped myself and said, "let me talk to Vince about this before you do anything."

I really didn't want to talk to Vince but I wanted to get to the bottom of it and also there was a part of me that could not believe it.

I met Vince for a cup of coffee and confronted him. At first he was in complete denial, then he said he was friends with her, "that's all", and then finally he admitted he had feelings for her. "What about your wife?", I asked him. He told me that he loved her too. I was incredulous and yelled "Do you realize you could lose her? What's wrong with you? You have to stop this right now. Stop going to the strip club and talk to your wife about it, or I will. I don't want her finding out from someone else."

Vince agreed to this and seemed remorseful.

Before all this happened I was getting worried that Valentina and Vince had been frequenting nightclubs on overtime, most weekends, and going to day parties after the night parties. Obviously partaking in party drugs to excess. I personally believe this is what lowered his morality bar. I found it a little strange that they wanted to go every weekend. Generally the regulars at these clubs are single and part of the fun was meeting potential partners. Even though it's great to be able to have fun together as a couple at these clubs - not every single weekend. As a couple, I want to spend some time just being a couple, just the two of us.

A few months later Valentina announced that it was over with her and her husband, Vince, because he had started dating a stripper! Yes they dated for a while, she wasn't being stalked, she was loving the attention.

My Girlfriend the Stripper…and Drugs

Valentina kept her dignity throughout this whole sordid experience, not saying too much in public or even to us girlfriends. She moved through the divorce with grace. None of us are friends with Vince since this betrayal and we feel to this day that he must regret losing this beautiful, amazing woman in his life. What a loser!

As soon as Linda had paid the debt she got out of the stripping business and moved on. She does not regret this experience in her life.

Chapter 14

A Waste of Life

My partner and I pulled our Divisional van into the car park of St.Kilda Police station a few minutes before the end of a long night shift. The sun was just beginning to come up and it was a cold, crisp, clear morning. I was tired and ready to go home, have a shower, wash the grime of the night off and crawl into bed, when our Sarge stopped us in the foyer. "Just got a report of a dead body at the Elwood canal." "Give it to the morning shift", my partner and I almost said in unison.

"There's fifteen minutes left of your shift."

"But Sarge, by the time we do the paperwork it will be lunch time", My partner complained.

"Well you better get a move on then," he said.

We pulled the van up near the location reported. A grassy strip between the canal and back fences of several homes. As we approached the small crowd of people - some dressed in pajamas and dressing gowns, a couple of joggers, a business man in a suit - they moved away to reveal a body of a young man, early twenties, face up, with several stab wounds.

One of the neighbors, in pajamas said, "I heard screaming near my back fence and by the time I came out to check, I saw the body." A few of the crowded nodded and murmured in agreement. The man in the business suit said, "I heard yelling then someone shouted, 'Die you bastard!' I raced towards the sounds and saw two young men, Asian, tall, skinny, long hair, running away in that direction, (pointing). They were both carrying, it looked like, large knives. There was also two girls with them, white girls."

I got closer to the body of the young man, looking at the numerous stab wounds. He was still breathing. I checked his pulse, faint but definitely alive. I yelled to my partner, who was closer to the Divisional Van, "Call the MICA unit!" (Mobile Intensive Care Unit service of the Ambulance Department).

I held the young man's hand and said, "You hang in there, the ambulance is on the way." My partner moved the crowd back and continued to ask questions as to what had occurred as we heard the approaching ambulance siren. The MICA unit arrived and took over.

I love ambulance drivers and especially this unit. Amazing under pressure. "Is he going to make it?" I asked one of the Ambulance Officers, as they began to move the young man off. He grimaced and gave me a look that I knew meant the odds were not good.

As the ambulance raced off we continued to question the crowd. A young man, in his early twenties ran up to us and said, "That's Mike, my friend. Is he going to be okay?"

The young man introduced himself as Pete and explained that about an hour earlier he had received a frantic phone call from his friend, Mike, who was hiding in a phone box. Mike had called him and told him that he thought he was in deep shit and that these two Filipino guys were after him, threatening to kill him. Pete said that his friend Mike sounded really scared and told him that these guys were crazy and they had big fucking Machetes, acting like Ninjas. Mike said he thought they weren't serious and then one of them just stabbed him in the arm. Pete said he told Mike to stay there and he would come get him. Mike started yelling, "I see them, oh fuck, they are coming, hurry please help me!"

Pete told us he had been driving around in a panic trying to find his friend when he heard the ambulance siren and followed it here, thinking it may be his friend. I asked him, "Do you know who these Filipino guys are and where we could find them?" Pete said he had met them before and been to their flat once. He thought he would be able to spot it again but didn't know the address. I asked him, "Do you know why these guys were after your friend?" Pete said it was something to do with the fact that Mike had borrowed one of their cars and had a minor accident and it escalated into some fight over that.

My partner and I got Pete to sit in the back of our van and we began to drive around Elwood to see if he could recognize where these two filipinos lived. We drove around for about ten minutes when Pete called out, "That's it, they live at the back of these flats, an apartment on the ground floor." Pete pointed out a seventies cream brick building.

We contacted VKC radio, requested back-up and got ready to raid the flat. By the time the back-up arrived a couple of reporters were on the scene. They scan our radios 24/7. We created a perimeter and kept the reporters and Pete back behind it as we took up position.

I will never forget the scene I witnessed as we burst through the front door of that flat. Two twenty-year-old

Filipino boys were sitting on an old couch, still holding onto their large machetes, covered in blood. Two seventeen-year-old bleach blonde haired girls in tight jeans and singlet tops, sat opposite them just watching in a kind of daze. One of the young men half attempted a stab at us as I yelled "Drop your knife now!" The girls began to scream, frozen on the spot.

The other filipino man leaped up and ran out the back door. He dropped the machete on the ground outside and was half way over the back fence, when he was grabbed by one of our colleagues.

Once back at the station, we contacted the detectives and brought them up-to-date as to what had occurred. Considering we basically apprehended the culprits immediately, the Detectives invited us to sit in on the interview and to interview the girls.

At lunchtime the detectives told the two filipinos they better start talking because they may be looking at murder charges. The report from the hospital was "it didn't look like he was going to make it".

The girls by this stage had been crying for some time. I'm sorry to say but they were stupid bimbos on vacation from Queensland. They had met the two filipinos at a bar and had been hooking up with them all weekend. They stood by at the canal watching while this poor young man was stabbed more than twenty times. It took me all my willpower to not slap them across the face several times. "Why didn't you try to stop them? Or at least run and call the police? You just stood by and watched?" All they could say was "I don't know."

The two filipino men seemed almost proud of their work. The story was they were friends of sorts with Mike and he needed to borrow a car while his was in the shop. He had a small 'fender bender'. A broken tail light, minor stuff and told the boys he couldn't pay to fix it at the moment. This escalated into a major argument and they insisted if he didn't pay immediately they would kill him. Mike thought this was ridiculous and told them, "Fuck you, I'm not gonna pay". They thought they were justified in what they did.

By this time it was 2pm in the afternoon and my partner and I had been working since 11pm the night before. We were exhausted and had to be back on night shift that night at 11pm again that night. The detectives and our Sergeant sent us home but not before we inquired how Mike was doing? They informed us he was in intensive care.

By the time we came back on nightshift at 11pm the two young Filipino men had been charged with murder. Mike , twenty years old, was pronounced dead earlier that evening at 7.00pm.

Chapter 15

Inappropriate Behavior

I was on nightshift, recently transferred to Stkilda Police station from South Melbourne and the passenger on the divisional van with my partner, the Senior Constable Jones, driving.

At that time St. Kilda was a highly sought after station as "a lot of action went on there" so most new cops wanted to be stationed there. Me, not necessarily.

I was beginning to settle in though and gaining respect from the fellow officers. I had become quite friendly with Senior Constable Jones. I enjoyed working with him. He seemed like a pretty cool cop, who knew his business and a happily married family man. When you work a few shifts together you begin to often develop camaraderie and get to know each other a little better. We had bonded over 'capturing' an 'escaped violent mental patient', known as "Sharky" and transporting him back to the Larundel Mental Institution'.

Larundel reminded me of a cross between the movie "One Flew Over The Cuckoos Nest" and a hotel resort. Driving through the grounds there were nice gardens and walking paths and various small apartment type buildings. Some of the low security patients wandered the grounds freely and could be seen sitting on benches etc, quite a normal looking scene.

Even the foyer, where we delivered the patients to a locked security door, looked like a pleasant hotel lobby, except for the maximum security locked door, where occasionally you could hear muffled screams.

We were called to the door, or directed there with our patient by a Doctor in a white coat and often when opened by staff, there were blood curdling screams coming from the inside.

Inappropriate Behavior

I once met a nurse, socially, who worked there and I thought her much braver than me. I think I must have delivered 'patients' there at least four times.

We were called to transfer the 'patients' the ambulance drivers refused to take, whenever there was a violent mental patient at the hospitals.

I remember arriving at Prince Alfred Hospital once, asking the nurse "Who are we taking?"

And she answered, pointing "The one strapped to the bed over there" I looked in the direction to see a scary looking man, convulsing and attempting to escape from his hospital bed.

Sharky the Regular Escape Artist

Sharky was a regular escape artist and the first time we got the call to look for him the radio operator on our van said "VKC St. Kilda 203 we have an escaped mental patient known as "Sharky", in the vicinity of Grey Street and Fitzroy Street. Approach with caution. He is known to be extremely violent."

I picked up the mouthpiece and answered the radio call. "Roger that VKC. Anything else to help us identify?"

The radio operator chuckled and said "Yeah he has two tattoos of sharks on his face."

We found him soon after on Grey street and approached him tentatively.

"Hi Sharky, how are you doing?" I said.

He hopped into the back of our divisional van without a peep and, docile and quiet as a mouse. Senior Constable Jones and I looked at each other. "Well that was easy".

On the drive out to Larundel he banged about in the back of the van and we keep calling to him. "Sharky you are going to hurt yourself if you don't sit still", to no avail.

Once we got to Larundel and got him out of the van, he was docile again and didn't seem to have any visible injuries from banging around in the back.

The process on arrival at Larundal Hospital is you enter the lobby and report to the reception desk, then the receptionist notifies the appropriate doctor to come get the patient.

Senior Constable Jones and I sat on an L-shaped lounge, Sharky, sitting quietly between us.

I was feeling a little uncomfortable already because a man, a few minutes earlier, introduced himself, "Hello I'm Doctor Smith," and before I could shake his outstretched hand, the Receptionist leaned out of her window and called out, "Fred, get back to your room and leave the nice police officers alone."

A few moments later another man came and sat next to me and spoke in a whisper, I had to lean in to him very close to hear him, "Hello how are you?" I answered politely, "Fine thanks." Sharky stared ahead blankly and Senior Constable Jones just grinned." The man then whispered again "You know I always wanted to be a cop." I answered "Oh that's nice". He whispered something else and as I leaned in to be able to hear him he screamed at the top of his lungs "So I could say "FREEZE YOU MOTHERFUCKER!"

My partner and I jumped up in fright, then began laughing at the shock as Sharky just sat there nonchalantly.

A few weeks later they changed this protocol of delivery after a patient grabbed a cop's gun as he sat on the couch and then shot himself right in front of the cop.

Not Normal Police Behavior Or #Metoo

It was a crisp cold night. The late night restaurants on Fitzroy Street Stkilda began to close up shop and the late night stragglers began to head home.

Senior Constable Jones pulled the divisional van into the car park behind the Fitzroy Street restaurant. The car park was almost empty and we headed towards the rear entrance where Senior Constable Jones parked the Divisional van and we both got out and headed towards a nearby group of men, surrounding a roast on a spit.

Senior Constable Jones said "Hi" to the friendly Restaurant owner and then introduced me to him and his cohorts. They were having some kind of celebration, can't remember what for but he offered us an alcoholic beverage and some food. I politely declined but Senior Constable Jones insisted so I took a drink rather than create a scene. I was a twenty year old female police trainee and if your 'senior on the van' tells you to do something you don't argue. Of course, I was worried we were drinking on duty, but it seemed like no one else was. After a little while we said our goodbyes and continued on our way.

I was feeling a little buzzed as 'Jones' drove the van along the foreshore and the sea mist rolled in. He drove along the pedestrian path heading towards Elwood. It must have been around 4.00am. He drove up close to a pedestrian bridge that crossed over the canal and to my shock he began to drive on to it.

I said "This is not a good idea, we've both been drinking and I'm not sure this bridge will hold a divisional van."

Jones ignored me and stopped in the middle of the bridge and turned off the ignition. I was thinking that maybe I should just get out but realized I could not open my passenger door as we were wedged on the bridge. Jones then began to move towards me and attempted to kiss me.

"What are you doing? I said. "You're married!" He just laughed and began to put his hand down my shirt and grabbed at my boob.

At first I attempted to half jokingly push him off saying "C'mon don't" and telling him to "stop" and "No, we shouldn't be doing this," but he kept pushing himself on me and trying to kiss me. He began to grab at my belt to try and undo it and I felt frozen in shock, squashed against my passenger door.

I couldn't believe what was happening. I attempted to push him off again and he was half laughing, "Come on it will be fun."

He kept saying things like that and getting more intense as I looked around in panic, feeling trapped against my passenger door. He began to get more aggressive as he groped at me and intensified his voice. "Just shut up!" I began to feel nauseous and said so.

"I think I'm going to be sick. Get off me." Jones suddenly seemed to sober up and he got off me.

He then muttered something along the lines of, "Don't tell anyone about this."

I, of course, did not and from that night on, he basically ignored me when we passed each other in the station house.

I felt equally disappointed by his sexual misconduct and the fact that 'this supposedly happily married family man' would try this on me and that he ruined a friendship of sorts and that he stopped talking to me. I was also sad that the respect for him was gone also.

Chapter 16

Bad Cop

I met Sally when I was a trainee at South Melbourne Station. She had thick beautiful blonde hair and could have easily been a model. She was very nice to me. Once when we were on night shift together she offered for me to sleep over at her place. She lived close to the station and we had finished late with a quick change over the next day.

I slept in her bed and found out sometime later that she was bisexual. I was slightly offended she didn't make a move on me, though if she had I would not have known what to do with myself.

A few weeks later Sally was off work with a broken jaw. I asked my Sarge what had happened, "Did they throw the book at the crook who did it?" My Sarge didn't say anything for a while so I pressed him. "Tell me, is she going to be okay?"

He then told me that her boyfriend, Max, did it. I couldn't believe it.

"Why?" I asked.

Apparently they had been at a cop barbecue and Sally was talking 'a little too close to another cop', Max got jealous and punched her right in front of everyone.

"Sarge, that's serious assault! Is he going to go to jail?"

My Sarge just looked at me blankly.

I insisted "that he needs to be charged" and "because he is a cop it's even worse".

My Sarge continued to explain to me that it would not be a good idea and after my insisting he told me that "Cops don't rat on other cops". He then told me a warning story of a young policewoman whistleblower. She had her badge stolen from her locker room and it was planted in a local brothel. The local prostitutes working at the brothel were paid to say that "the young policewoman worked there part-time" and soon after she was dismissed from the police force.

I proceeded to tell my Sarge. "That's ridiculous. No one would believe that story and if it happened to me I could prove my innocence."

My Sarge said "Sure in the end you would but that story would be out there for ever."

I often think back about some of these instances and wish I had done something about them, stood up, or knew how to make a difference. At the time, being a young trainee in my 20's I didn't have the maturity or understanding or know-how, or maybe the guts to stand up and be counted. I admire the courage of anyone who does.

I had worked with Sally's boyfriend once before. He was a real asshole. As soon as I got into the police car with him to start the shift he said "Sit there and shut up and don't touch the radio."

Years later when he came to work at my local station I told my Roster Sarge, "Don't every put me on the roster with him. I will never work a shift with him so don't even think about it!"

Chapter 17

Drunk Drivers and a Cop Goes to Jail

One of my least favorite duties as a cop was working at a breathalyzer testing station on a Saturday night. I would rather be coming or going to a party, like the Drivers I tested, instead of standing out in the cold conducting breathalyzer tests.

I have stupidly driven before, when I was over the limit, and contrary to what you think at the time, our senses are affected and our response times are slower. A vehicle can become a lethal weapon when driving with a lack of concentration. Today, texting and being on your phone is just as bad.

For a short time I shared an apartment with a beautiful young policewoman a few years senior to me. Jane could have easily been a full-time model. Long blonde hair, tall, slim and flawless skin with angular features. Jane was very popular and we got on well.

Jane's boyfriend was an obnoxious alcoholic detective. Very jealous and possessive of Jane. I could not understand what she saw in him, she could do so much better.

Whenever Jane's boyfriend arrived at our flat he sucked all the energy out of the room. If he even acknowledged my existence, it would be a gruff, "Hello", before he would disappear behind closed doors with Jane.

One early morning Jane came into my room and woke me up in tears. Jane informed me that her boyfriend had been arrested.

Apparently he had a traffic accident where he slammed into the back of a stationary vehicle at a red light. He must have been going very fast because the impact caused the death of a 19-year-old male.

Drunk Drivers and a Cop Goes to Jail

The police arrived and Jane's boyfriend apparently refused a breathalyzer test at the scene and physically fought the cops. He was taken to the hospital for a blood test, where he fought the hospital staff also. He was charged with resisting arrest and vehicular manslaughter. His blood alcohol reading was way over the limit.

The whole time during the trial, and even when he was convicted and sentenced to prison, Jane's boyfriend showed no signs of remorse at causing the death of a young man. He was only worried about who he might come into contact with in prison, possibly someone he had "put away".

For some reason Jane stuck by him, visiting him regularly in the low security prison farm a few hundred miles away in country Victoria. I lost touch with Jane over the years, but the last I heard many years ago was that they were engaged.

One of the worst things I had to do as a cop, for me, was attending car accidents, some fatal. Seeing mangled bodies and thinking that this person, people, were just driving along a few minutes before, maybe singing along to the radio, contemplating what they were going to have for lunch or dinner, having no idea that in a few moments their life would be taken so quickly and harshly.

Chapter 18

My Biggest Arrest

I was the senior person on the van, at twenty five years old with my brand new trainee by my side, Ed, who was twenty five himself. We were on an early morning shift. It was 7.30 am a crisp Sunday spring morning and the sea mist had just lifted to expose a beautiful blue sky.

Driving down Fitzroy St, it was very quiet, all the restaurants and hotels closed. No one on the sidewalks.

I noticed further down the street a man walking by himself and as we got closer I could see he was an Aboriginal, looking around hesitantly, as he carried a large object. I pulled the van up beside him and motioned to Ed, my partner, the trainee, to hop out with me.

"Good morning". I said "What brings you out and about so early and what do you have there with you?"

The Aboriginal man held his hands behind his back, seemingly hiding something.

"Let's see it," I said. Finally, he showed us. It was a large, professional, expensive-looking camera.

"Where did you get that?" I asked

"Found it" he said.

"What's your name?" "Simon Black" he said.

We both raised our eyebrows at this. An Aboriginal called Black. That's a first.

My Biggest Arrest

"Okay, Simon, we will hang on to the camera for now. Hop in the back of the van and we are going down the station for a chat." Slowly, but obediently, he got in the back of the van.

As we drove towards the station I called into the back of the van.

"Simon, by the time we get back to the station I want to know how and where you stole that camera from, okay?"

My new trainee whispered "Aren't we supposed to read him his rights, say "You are not obliged to say anything unless —".

"That's only in the movies, and besides we haven't arrested him yet," I replied.

My trainee got a huge crush on me that day. He thought I was 'a super cop' because it turned out in fact that Simon had just climbed into a lovely Stkilda home's open window about an hour earlier and taken the camera from the coffee table of a local resident.

There was a label attached to the camera with the name of the owner. When we called him, he had just woken up and said "yes the camera belonged to him" and he went into his lounge room and was shocked to find out that a man had been wandering around his house while he was asleep an hour earlier.

I knew I had just got lucky seeing him walking along the street with the camera, it just didn't fit the picture and I said, "Okay Simon I know you have done at least three other burglaries recently. Why don't you tell me about them?" And he actually did!

We spent the afternoon driving around the streets as he pointed out houses that he had burgled and we solved a number of crimes that day. Simon Black pointed out houses he had stolen VCRS, TV sets, boom box radios etc. In total, six houses and he also gave up his 'fence', the guy who got rid of these stolen goods for him.

As we began the interrogations our local detectives paid a visit. They normally take over at this stage but they said "You can do this one because Simon has been in and out of jail many times and normally says nothing at all when he's arrested so you go for it."

I asked Simon later why he told me everything and he said "cause I didn't give him a wack across the ears and I talked nice to him."

There was a group of local homeless Aborigines at that time that congregated in the Cattani Gardens by the foreshore and drank copious amounts of cheap alcohol out of brown paper bags and then fell asleep in the grass. Most were harmless and just displaced citizens.

The history of the Aboriginals in Australia and the way they were treated is not something our country should be proud of.

They are a nomadic people that were introduced to western ways through alcohol, disease and attempts to urbanize. Generally aborigines are alcohol intolerant which also doesn't help.

Around the time of arresting Simon there was a huge national incident that made the front page of every newspaper.

There was a local trendy bar in Fitzroy Street, named the 'Cattani Bar' just like the local park at the foreshore at the end of the street. The owner refused to serve a man he thought was one of the local homeless Aboriginal drunks and sent him out of his bar. Unfortunately, the owner did not recognize this slightly drunk Aboriginal who just happened to be a famous Aboriginal singer with a number one hit record.

The singer made a national incident out of it and a few weeks later the bar was closed for good.

Chapter 19

Sliding Doors

Charlie played football for a few more years then continued working as a chef. He then gave that up and became a carpenter, building houses and buying real estate and doing very well. We had two beautiful blonde-haired, blued-eyed children, a boy and then a girl. We had a comfortable four bedroom home with an in-ground pool, in Beaumaris, a bayside suburb of Melbourne.

I continued to build my career in the police force, moving through the ranks with time off here and there for maternity leave and long service leave where we did some amazing trips to Europe and America. The kids got to come with us on some, seeing Disneyland and The Grand Canyon and the bright lights of New York City.

Charlie and I went on a few romantic trips just for us too, when our friends or the grandparents looked after our kids, Tom and Sarah. They are good kids.

Tom is studying to be a doctor and has a great group of friends, a steady girlfriend and he is a kind soul.

Sarah is a physical therapist and loves it. She also has a steady boyfriend, yes he's an AFL footballer with a sports psychology background, smart and kind.

I am currently in the Public Relations Department of the Victoria Police Force with rumors, if I want to, one day become the Chief Commissioner. I'm mostly behind a desk these days and I must admit, I enjoy it.

We have a good life, great circle of friends and my husband, the father of my children loves me and treats me with respect. I think we will leave a fine legacy. Good kind children who will bring up their children the same way.

No... that's not what happened

I broke up with Charlie because I wanted to take on the world, have experiences, try new things, new people, rise up the ladder, live in different countries. I was too young too be tied down and live a suburban life.

And I did... I lived in London for five years, went to all the hottest night clubs and private members clubs, the best restaurants, saw amazing theatre and had regular trips to Paris, France and Italy. I dated a billionaire, actors, a plastic surgeon, a model, men with titles and royal links, a movie producer, director and an architect. French, Italian, Bulgarian, Iranian, British, American, African American, Black, Brown, Caucasian.

I lived in New York and then Los Angeles. I have beautiful friends from England and China and France and Sweden and Denmark and Switzerland and Austria and Mexico, who live all over the world in London and France and Spain and Italy and Thailand and Bali and Hong Kong and Singapore and Mexico City. I have lived in London, New York and then Los Angeles.

I get up every morning and I feel alive. I occasionally reminisce about what might have been with Charlie, I might have been happy that way too...

Epilogue

Charlie married a South American girl with a sweet smile and they have a beautiful child. They live in Miami and we are still friends on Facebook.

I reside just under the Hollywood sign in Los Angeles. I am engaged in a committed relationship, no children and no plans to set a wedding date. We do talk about fostering or adopting one day.

I have eleven wonderful nieces and nephews from age eighteen months to twenty four, seven brothers and sisters, two mums and dads...

About the Author

Wendy Wilkins is an award winning actress, writer, filmmaker based in Los Angeles. Wendy is honored to have recently become an American citizen having lived here for years via London, originally from Australia. After being a young cop, Wendy became one of the most successful Real estate agents in Australia, personally selling over a Billion dollars in sales. Her creative passions kept calling her since she put shows on for her grandfather in her garage when she was a little girl. The joy on his face still resonates with Wendy today. Wendy has won awards on the festival circuit and been delighted to act in a number of award winning films and TV shows. Wendy also has a number of screenplays in various forms of development.

www.ingramcontent.com/pod-product-compliance
Lightning Source LLC
Chambersburg PA
CBHW031421290426
44110CB00011B/476